Caring for Your Castle

A Guide for Home Ownership

This book is dedicated to Denny Brandt, a man whose integrity and compassion have helped countless families achieve their piece of the American Dream. Through his unwavering dedication and assistance, he has turned the dream of homeownership into reality for many, embodying the spirit of community and support. May this guide serve as a testament to his enduring impact and commitment to helping others build their futures, one home at a time.

amazon.com/author/tiofelipe

First published by Tio Felipe Designs 2024
https://www.tiofelipe.com/

Copyright © February 2024 by Tio Felipe

All rights reserved. No part of this publication may be reproduced, stored or transmitted in any form or by any means, electronic, mechanical, photocopying, recording, scanning, or otherwise without written permission from the publisher. It is illegal to copy this book, post it to a website, or distribute it by any other means without permission.

First edition

Dear Reader,

Thank you for choosing this book! If you enjoyed it, we kindly ask you to take a moment and share your thoughts by writing a review on Amazon. Your feedback helps us improve and reach more readers.

We appreciate your support and look forward to hearing about your experience with the book.

Happy reading!

Tío Felipe
www.amazon.com/author/tiofelipe

Caring for Your Castle

A Guide for Home Ownership

Contents

Introduction to Home Maintenance	3
Understanding Your Home	5
Seasonal Maintenance Checklists	9
Basic Repairs and DIY Maintenance	13
Preventive Measures	17
Maintenance Schedules for Inside Your Home	21
Maintenance Schedules for Outside Your Home	25
Pest Control	29
Emergency Preparedness	33
Home Improvement and Enhancements	37
Resources	41
Conclusion	45

APPENDICES

How to Clean Gutters and Downspouts	48
How to Test Smoke and Carbon Monoxide Detectors	50
How to Seal Windows and Doors	52
How to Flush a Water Heater	55
Checking and Replacing the Water Heater Anode Rod	57
How to Change HVAC Air Filters	59
How to Fix a Leaky Faucet	61
How to Unclog Drains	63
How to Patch and Repair Drywall	65
How to Care for Lawn and Garden	67
How to Maintain a Deck or Patio	70
How to Remove Gum from Carpet	72
Monthly Maintenance Checklist	75
Seasonal Maintenance Checklists	76
Annual Maintenance Checklist	80
Home Safety and Security Checklist	81
Energy Efficiency Checklist	82
Must-Know Hacks for a Better Home Life	83

"A man's home is his castle."

—Benjamin Franklin

Introduction to Home Maintenance

Welcome to your guide to home maintenance, a practical resource designed for homeowners at every stage, whether you've just turned the key in your first home or been nesting for years. This guide is built on the understanding that a well-maintained home is the cornerstone of a comfortable, safe, and efficient living space. It's not just about fixing what's broken; it's about preventative measures that keep minor issues from becoming big problems.

Homeownership comes with its joys and challenges. One of the ongoing responsibilities is maintaining the property. This might seem daunting, especially for new homeowners navigating the complexities of property upkeep for the first time. However, even seasoned homeowners face new maintenance challenges as home technologies and standards evolve.

Why Maintenance Matters

Regular maintenance extends the life of your home's components, systems, and appliances. It's about protecting your investment, ensuring your living space is safe, and keeping your home running efficiently to save on energy costs. Maintenance can help avoid large, unexpected repair bills by catching problems early.

How to Use This Guide

This guide is structured to help you better understand your home, with easy-to-follow maintenance schedules, DIY repair instructions, and tips for when to call the professionals. It's designed to be flexible, allowing you to adapt the information to suit your home's needs and local climate.

Customizing Your Maintenance Schedule

Every home is unique, and so is every climate. That's why it's important to customize this guide's recommendations to fit your situation. For example, a home in a humid coastal region might require more frequent checks for rust and mold than in a dry, desert area. Similarly, the age and condition of your home might necessitate adjustments to the suggested maintenance routines.

As you read this guide, consider listing tasks specific to your home. This might include annual servicing of your HVAC system, semi-annual gutter cleaning, or monthly checks of your home's safety devices. Establishing a personalized home maintenance calendar will help you keep track of these tasks and ensure nothing gets overlooked.

In the following sections, we'll dive into the details of maintaining your home, covering everything from seasonal maintenance checklists to emergency preparedness. Whether you're fixing a leaky faucet, preparing your home for winter, or planning a major renovation, this guide is here to support you every step of the way.

Remember, maintaining your home is not just about preserving its value; it's about creating a space where you and your family can live comfortably and safely for years. Let's get started.

Understanding Your Home

To effectively maintain your home, it's crucial to have a solid understanding of its fundamental systems and components. This knowledge will empower you to perform regular inspections, identify potential issues early, and manage your maintenance tasks efficiently. Here, we'll cover the basics of your home's critical systems—HVAC, plumbing, and electrical—provide you with checklists for regular inspections, and guide you on setting up a personalized maintenance calendar.

Basic Home Systems

1. **HVAC (Heating, Ventilation, and Air Conditioning):**
   - Purpose: Keeps your home comfortable year-round, ensures good air quality, and regulates humidity levels.
   - Key Components:
     o Heating: Furnace or boiler, radiators or heating panels.
     o Ventilation: Ductwork, air filters, and exhaust fans.
     o Air Conditioning: Central AC, evaporator coils, and condensing units.
   - Maintenance Tips:
     o Replace or clean air filters every 1-3 months to ensure efficiency and good air quality.
     o Schedule annual professional inspections for heating and cooling systems before peak seasons.
     o Keep outdoor units free from debris and vegetation to ensure proper airflow.

2. **Plumbing:**
   - Purpose: Provides fresh water to your home and removes wastewater.

- Key Components:
  - Water Supply: Pipes that bring water into your home.
  - Drain-Waste-Vent (DWV) System: Removes waste water and gases from your home.
  - Fixtures: Sinks, toilets, showers, and faucets.
- Maintenance Tips:
  - Regularly inspect for leaks in faucets, under sinks, and around appliances like dishwashers and refrigerators.
  - Know the location of the main water shut-off valve in emergencies.
  - Prevent clogs by avoiding the disposal of problematic items down drains and toilets.

3. **Electrical System:**
   - Purpose: Powers your appliances, lighting, and electronic devices.
   - Key Components:
     - Service Panel: Distributes electricity throughout your home via circuits.
     - Outlets and Switches: Access points for electrical power.
     - Wiring: Connects the electrical grid to your home's appliances and fixtures.
   - Maintenance Tips:
     - Test smoke detectors and carbon monoxide detectors monthly; replace batteries annually.
     - Ensure that outlets near water sources are equipped with Ground Fault Circuit Interrupters (GFCIs).
     - Look out for signs of electrical issues, such as flickering lights, frequent breaker trips, or outlets that are hot to the touch.

Regular Inspection Checklists

Monthly:
- Test smoke/carbon monoxide detectors.
- Inspect HVAC air filters and replace them if they are dirty.
- Check under sinks for leaks.
- Ensure that electrical outlets and switches are functioning correctly.

Quarterly:
- Test garage door auto-reverse feature.
- Check the water softener and add salt if needed.
- Inspect and possibly flush out the water heater to remove sediment.

Bi-Annually:
- Deep clean your home to extend the life of appliances and surfaces.
- Vacuum refrigerator coils to improve efficiency.
- Check your home's exterior for signs of damage or wear.

Annually:
- Have HVAC systems serviced by a professional.
- Inspect roofing for damage, leaks, or missing shingles.
- Clean gutters and downspouts to prevent water damage.

Setting Up a Maintenance Calendar

Creating a personalized home maintenance calendar helps you stay organized and ensures that you don't overlook essential tasks. Here's how to set one up:

1. **List Tasks:** List all maintenance tasks required for your home, categorized by frequency (monthly, quarterly, bi-annually, annually).

2. **Use a Digital Calendar:** Input these tasks into a digital calendar of your choice. Set reminders a few days before each task to give yourself time to prepare.

3. **Adjust as Needed:** Your home's needs may change

over time, so be prepared to adjust your calendar. After completing a task, please take note of its condition and anticipate future maintenance needs.

4. **Include Seasonal Maintenance:** Include seasonal maintenance tasks into your calendar. This ensures that your home is prepared for the changing weather conditions throughout the year.

By understanding your home's essential systems, conducting regular inspections, and setting up a maintenance calendar, you can keep your home running smoothly and efficiently. This proactive approach prevents costly repairs and ensures a safe and comfortable living environment for you and your family.

Seasonal Maintenance Checklists

Maintaining your home requires a year-round commitment, with each season bringing its own set of tasks to ensure your property remains in top condition. These seasonal maintenance checklists will help you track what needs to be done to protect your investment and ensure your home's safety and efficiency.

Spring

1. **Exterior Inspection** (Roof, Siding, Foundation):
   - Roof: Look for missing, loose, or damaged shingles and leaks.
   - Siding: Check for cracks, damage, or signs of moisture.
   - Foundation: Inspect for cracks or signs of movement. Ensure soil slopes away from the foundation for proper drainage.

2. **Landscaping and Yard Maintenance**:
   - Prune trees and shrubs to encourage healthy growth.
   - Apply mulch to garden beds to help retain moisture and suppress weeds.
   - Start your lawn care routine, including aeration, seeding, and fertilizing.

3. **HVAC System Service**:
   - Schedule professional servicing for your HVAC system to ensure it's ready for the cooling season.
   - Clean or replace air filters to maintain air quality and system efficiency.

4. **Pest Control Measures:**
   - Inspect your home for signs of pests, paying close attention to areas where you've had issues.
   - Seal up entry points to prevent insects and rodents from entering.
   - Consider professional pest control services if necessary.

Summer

1. **Window and Door Checks for Leaks:**
   - Inspect seals and weatherstripping around windows and doors. Replace any that are damaged to improve energy efficiency.

2. **Gutter Cleaning and Repairs:**
   - Clean out gutters and downspouts to prevent water damage. Repair any leaks or loose sections.

3. **Deck and Patio Maintenance:**
   - Inspect decks and patios for signs of wear or damage. Clean, seal, or stain wood surfaces to protect them from the elements.

4. **Sprinkler System Check:**
   - Test your sprinkler system and adjust heads for proper coverage. Repair any leaks or broken components.

Fall

1. **Heating System Service:**
   Have your heating system serviced by a professional to ensure it's in working order before the cold weather arrives.

2. **Chimney and Fireplace Inspection:**
   Hire a professional to clean and inspect your chimney and fireplace to prevent chimney fires and carbon monoxide poisoning.

3. **Sealing Gaps and Leaks in Doors and Windows:**
   Apply caulk or weatherstripping to seal leaks, reducing drafts and lowering heating costs.

4. **Preparing Your Home for Winter**:
   - Drain and store hoses and shut off outdoor water valves to prevent freezing.
   - Cover air conditioners and remove or secure window units.
   - Insulate pipes in vulnerable areas to prevent freezing.

Winter

1. **Indoor Air Quality Checks**:
   - Replace furnace filters to maintain indoor air quality.
   - Consider using a humidifier to add moisture to dry winter air.

2. **Pipe Insulation to Prevent Freezing**:
   - Insulate exposed pipes in basements, attics, and garages to prevent freezing.

3. **Roof and Gutter Checks for Ice Dams**:
   - Inspect the roof for ice dams or icicles, indicating inadequate insulation or ventilation in the attic.
   - Clean gutters to ensure proper drainage.

4. **Emergency Kit Updates for Winter Storms**:
   - Check and update your home's emergency kit with supplies like batteries, flashlights, a first aid kit, and non-perishable food items.
   - Include cold-weather essentials like blankets, warm clothing, and a portable heater if possible.

By following these seasonal maintenance checklists, you can systematically address the needs of your home throughout the year, ensuring it remains safe, comfortable, and efficient no matter the season.

"The ache for home lives in all of us. The safe place where we can go as we are and not be questioned."

—Maya Angelou

Basic Repairs and DIY Maintenance

Tackling basic repairs and maintenance tasks around the house can save homeowners time and money, not to mention the satisfaction of keeping their homes in top condition. Here are practical steps and tips for everyday DIY maintenance tasks, including plumbing, electrical work, drywall repair, and floor maintenance.

Fixing Leaky Faucets and Running Toilets

Leaky Faucets:
- Identify the Type of Faucet: Common types include compression, cartridge, ball, and disc faucets.
- Turn Off the Water Supply: Locate the valves under the sink and turn them clockwise to shut off the water.
- Disassemble the Faucet: Use a wrench and screwdriver to remove the faucet handle and other parts carefully. Keep track of the order and orientation for reassembly.
- Inspect and Replace Damaged Parts: Look for worn-out seals, O-rings, or washers. Take the damaged part to a hardware store to find an exact replacement.
- Reassemble and Test: Put the faucet back together and turn the water supply back on. Check for leaks and ensure smooth operation.

Running Toilets:
- Adjust the Fill Valve: If the water in the tank is too high and spilling into the overflow tube, adjust the fill valve to lower the water level.
- Inspect the Flapper: A worn flapper can cause water to leak from the tank into the bowl. Turn off the water, drain

the tank, and inspect the flapper. Replace it if it's worn or damaged.
- Check the Flush Valve and Handle: Make sure the flush handle mechanism is not sticking or overly tight, which can prevent the flapper from sealing correctly.

Basic Electrical Safety and Light Fixture Replacement

Safety First:
- Always turn off the power at the circuit breaker before starting any electrical work.
- Use a voltage tester to ensure the wires are not live before touching them.

Light Fixture Replacement:
- Remove the Old Fixture: Unscrew the mounting screws or nuts that hold the fixture to the ceiling or wall. Carefully disconnect the wires.
- Connect the New Fixture: Match the wire colors (usually black to black, white to white) and twist them together using wire connectors. Attach the ground wire to the grounding screw.
- Secure the Fixture: Mount the new fixture according to the manufacturer's instructions. Turn the power back on and test the fixture.

Drywall Repair and Painting Tips

Drywall Repair:
- For small holes, use spackle with a putty knife to fill the hole, then sand smooth once dry.
- For larger holes, you may need a patch kit or a piece of drywall, joint compound, and tape to cover and blend the repair into the surrounding area.

Painting Tips:
- Clean and sand the surface before painting to ensure the paint adheres properly.
- Use painter's tape to protect trim and ceilings for clean lines.
- Apply primer before painting, especially for new drywall or dark color changes. Use a roller for large areas and a brush for details.

Floor Maintenance (Carpet, Hardwood, Tile)

Carpet:
- Vacuum regularly to remove dirt and debris.
- Treat stains immediately with appropriate carpet cleaner.
- Consider professional cleaning annually, depending on traffic and use.

Hardwood:
- Use a soft broom or vacuum to remove dirt. Avoid excessive water when cleaning.
- Apply hardwood floor cleaner with a microfiber mop for deeper cleaning.
- Polish floors periodically and refinish every 3-5 years as needed.

Tile:
- Sweep or vacuum to remove loose dirt. Mop with a mild detergent solution.
- Clean grout lines with a grout cleaner or a baking soda paste for a DIY solution.
- Seal grout lines every 1-2 years to prevent staining and moisture absorption.

By mastering these essential repairs and maintenance tasks, homeowners can keep their living spaces functional and inviting while preserving their homes' value.

"Show me a family who owns their own home and I will show you the hope and future of America."

—Franklin D. Roosevelt

Preventive Measures to Keep Your Home in Top Condition

Preventive maintenance is vital to preserving the integrity and efficiency of your home. Adopting a proactive approach can avoid costly repairs, enhance your living environment, and improve your home's energy efficiency. Here are some essential preventive measures along with practical how-tos.

Regular Cleaning Schedules

Establish Routine Cleaning Tasks:
- Daily: Wipe down surfaces, do dishes, and manage clutter to keep spaces tidy and functional.
- Weekly: Vacuum and mop floors, clean bathrooms, and dust all surfaces to reduce allergens.
- Monthly: Clean vents, dust light fixtures and ceiling fans, and vacuum upholstery to maintain air quality and prolong the life of fabrics.

Deep Cleaning:
- Schedule bi-annual deep cleans in the spring and fall to address areas not part of your regular cleaning routine, such as behind appliances, inside the oven, and windows.

Detecting and Addressing Mold and Mildew

Prevention and Detection:
- Ventilation: Ensure adequate ventilation in high-moisture areas like bathrooms and kitchens to prevent mold growth.

- Humidity Control: Use dehumidifiers in damp areas and maintain indoor humidity levels between 30-50%.
- Inspection: Regularly inspect for signs of mold or mildew in dark, damp places, windows, and under sinks.

Addressing Mold:
- For small areas, clean mold with water and detergent. Avoid using bleach, if possible, as it doesn't prevent mold from returning and can harm your health.
- For larger infestations, consider hiring a professional mold remediation service to ensure it is appropriately and safely removed.

Reducing Clutter and Improving Home Organization

Clutter Control:
- Adopt a "one in, one out" policy to prevent accumulating unnecessary items.
- Regularly donate or sell items you no longer need or use.

Organization Systems:
- Implement storage solutions that fit your space and lifestyle, such as shelving units, drawer organizers, and labeled bins.
- Use digital tools or a household binder to keep track of warranties, manuals, and maintenance schedules.

Energy Efficiency Tips

Insulation and Sealing:
- Check and upgrade insulation in critical areas such as the attic, walls, and floors to maintain comfortable temperatures and reduce energy bills.
- Seal gaps and leaks around doors, windows, and where utility lines enter the house to prevent air leaks.

Energy-Efficient Lighting:
- Replace incandescent bulbs with LED lights, which use at least 75% less energy and last 25 times longer.
- Consider intelligent lighting systems that can be controlled remotely and programmed to reduce energy consumption.

Appliance Use and Maintenance:
- Ensure appliances are energy-efficient models and keep them well-maintained (e.g., cleaning refrigerator coils, setting appropriate temperatures).
- Use programmable thermostats to optimize heating and cooling schedules, reducing energy use when you're not home.

Implementing these preventive measures can significantly contribute to keeping your home in top condition, safeguarding against potential issues, and enhancing overall comfort and efficiency. Regular attention to cleaning, mold prevention, clutter reduction, and energy conservation maintains the aesthetic appeal of your home and contributes to a healthy and sustainable living environment.

"Home is the nicest word there is."

—Laura Ingalls Wilder

Maintenance Schedules for Inside Your Home

Keeping the interior of your home in good condition involves routine maintenance of its systems and appliances. Regular upkeep helps prevent breakdowns, increases efficiency, and ensures safety. Here are detailed guidelines for maintaining critical components inside your home.

Appliance Maintenance (Cleaning Filters, Checking Hoses)

Refrigerators and Freezers:
- Frequency: Clean coils every six months to maintain efficiency. Check door seals annually to ensure they are airtight.
- How-To: Use a coil brush and vacuum to clean the coils. Wipe down the seals with a mild detergent solution.

Washing Machines and Dryers:
- Frequency: Inspect hoses for leaks or bulges annually. Clean dryer vents, lint filters with every use, and deep clean vents annually.
- How-To: Replace rubber hoses with more durable stainless steel braided hoses. Clean the lint filter after each cycle and use a vent cleaning brush kit for the dryer vent.

Dishwashers:
- Frequency: Clean filters and check spinning arms monthly; inspect hoses annually.

- How-To: Remove the filter and wash it under running water. Check spinning arms for clogs and clear holes with a toothpick.

Ovens and Ranges:
- Frequency: Clean or replace filters in range hoods or over-the-stove microwaves every 3 to 6 months.
- How-To: For self-cleaning ovens, follow the manufacturer's instructions. For others, use a cleaner and scrub pad. Soak filters from hoods in a degreasing solution, then rinse and dry.

Checking and Replacing Smoke and Carbon Monoxide Detectors

- Frequency: Test monthly, replace batteries at least once a year, and replace units every ten years or as the manufacturer recommends.
- How-To: Press the test button to ensure the alarm sounds. Use the end of a broom handle if the button isn't easily reachable. When replacing batteries, open the compartment, replace it with new batteries, and close it securely. For unit replacement, detach the detector from its mounting bracket, disconnect the power (if hardwired), and install a new unit following the manufacturer's instructions.

HVAC Filter Replacement

- Frequency: Replace or clean filters every 1-3 months, depending on the type of filter and your household's needs (e.g., pets, allergies).
- How-To: Locate the filter slot, remove the old filter, and note the size and direction of airflow indicated on the edge. Insert the new filter with the airflow direction aligned correctly. Clean reusable filters with water and let them dry completely before reinstalling.

Plumbing Checks for Leaks and Clogs

- Frequency: Perform visual inspections for leaks under sinks and around toilets and water heaters annually. Check for slow drains as they occur.

- How-To:
    - Leaks: Look for wet spots, drips, or signs of water damage. Tighten fittings or replace worn parts as needed.
    - Clogs: Use a plunger for simple clogs. A drain snake or mixing baking soda and vinegar can help clear drains for persistent issues. Avoid chemical drain cleaners as they can damage pipes.

By adhering to these maintenance schedules and performing these tasks regularly, you can ensure the systems and appliances inside your home operate smoothly, prevent costly repairs, and maintain a safe and comfortable living environment.

"Owning a home lies at the very heart of the idea of the American Dream."

—Henry Bonilla

Maintenance Schedules for Outside Your Home

Maintaining your home's exterior enhances curb appeal and protects your investment against the elements. Regular upkeep of your lawn, landscaping, the building's facade, and other outdoor features is crucial. Here are detailed maintenance schedules and tips for keeping the outside of your home in excellent condition.

Lawn Care and Landscaping

Weekly Maintenance:
- Mowing: Keep your lawn at an ideal height, which varies by grass type but generally is about 2-3 inches to promote healthy roots.
- Weeding: Remove weeds regularly to prevent them from competing with your lawn and garden plants for nutrients and water.

Seasonal Tasks:
- Spring: Aerate your lawn to improve nutrient and water absorption. Apply pre-emergent weed control and fertilize.
- Summer: Increase watering during dry periods, and consider mulching to retain soil moisture.
- Fall: Rake leaves and aerate if needed. This is also a good time for overseeding to fill in bare spots.
- Winter: Minimize foot traffic on dormant grass to prevent damage.

Exterior Painting and Siding Care

Routine Checks:
- Inspect your home's exterior annually for chipping, peeling, or fading paint. Look for signs of damage or rot in siding materials.

Painting Schedule:
- Most homes must be repainted every 5-10 years, depending on the climate, the quality of the previous paint job, and the siding material.

Siding Maintenance:
- Vinyl: Clean annually with a mild soap solution and a soft brush to remove dirt and mildew.
- Wood: Besides painting, check for rot or insect damage and replace affected areas.
- Brick: Inspect mortar joints and repair any deterioration to prevent water intrusion.

Driveway and Walkway Maintenance

Regular Cleaning:
- Clean driveways and walkways with a pressure washer or hose to remove dirt, grime, and mildew at least once a year.

Crack Repair:
- Inspect for cracks or uneven sections annually. Use concrete or asphalt filler to repair cracks and prevent water from causing further damage.

Sealing:
- Seal concrete and asphalt driveways every 2-3 years to protect against weathering and cracking.

Fencing Repairs and Maintenance

Inspection and Cleaning:
- Inspect fences at least once a year for loose boards, rust (on metal fences), and damage from insects or moisture.
- Clean your fence annually with a pressure washer or specialized cleaner to remove dirt and mildew.

Repairs:
- Tighten loose screws and nails. Replace damaged or rotted boards promptly to prevent further damage to the structure.

Painting and Staining:
- Wooden fences should be painted or stained every 2-5 years to protect against the weather and UV damage.

By following these maintenance schedules for the outside of your home, you can ensure that your property looks its best and is protected from environmental damage. Regular upkeep can prevent minor issues from becoming costly repairs, preserving the beauty and value of your home.

home

"There's no place like home."

—The Wizard of Oz

Pest Control

Effective pest control is crucial to home maintenance, ensuring your living environment remains healthy and comfortable. Understanding the types of pests that can invade your home, implementing preventative measures, and knowing when to seek professional help is essential in managing pest issues.

Identifying Common Household Pests

Ants: Look for trails leading to food sources or water. Check for nests in walls or other dark, undisturbed places.

Cockroaches: Spot them in kitchens and bathrooms, especially at night. Look for droppings or egg cases in dark, secluded areas.

Rodents: Mice and rats leave droppings near food sources or nesting areas. Listen for scratching sounds in walls or attics, and check for chewed wires or food packages.

Termites: Look for wood damage, mud tubes on exterior walls, or wings from swarmers. Termites can cause significant damage before they are even detected.

Bed Bugs: Identify them by small, itchy bites and tiny blood spots on bedding. Check seams of mattresses and furniture crevices.

Preventative Measures for Pest Control

Seal Entry Points: Fill cracks and gaps in walls, around windows, and doors, including utility and pipe entrances, to prevent pest entry.

Eliminate Water Sources: Fix leaky faucets and pipes. Ensure good drainage at the foundation. Pests like cockroaches and mosquitoes thrive in moist environments.

Keep It Clean: Store food in sealed containers and dispose of garbage regularly. Clean crumbs and spills promptly so as not to attract pests.

Declutter: Reduce clutter to eliminate hiding spots for pests—store items in sealed plastic containers rather than cardboard boxes.

Maintain the Yard: Trim shrubbery and branches away from the house. Keep mulch, woodpiles, and debris away from the home's foundation to reduce shelter for pests.

Use Proper Lighting: Insects are less attracted to yellow or sodium vapor lights. Use these outside entrances or in the yard to reduce attracting pests.

When to Call a Professional Pest Control Service

Persistent Infestation: If DIY methods fail and pests continue to reappear, it may indicate a more extensive, hidden infestation.

Hazardous Pests: Certain pests, such as termites, bedbugs, or carpenter ants, require specialized treatment that DIY methods cannot effectively address.

Health Risks: Pests like rodents, cockroaches, and mosquitoes can pose health risks. Professional services can ensure these are managed safely and effectively.

Preventative Maintenance: Some homeowners opt for regular professional pest control services as a preventative measure, especially in areas prone to specific infestations.

Professional pest control services offer the advantage of experience and access to more effective treatment options that aren't available over the counter. They can also provide a customized approach based on the specific type of pests and the extent of the infestation, ensuring the problem is resolved efficiently and with minimal risk to your health and home.

By staying vigilant and proactive with these pest control strategies, homeowners can significantly reduce the likelihood of infestations and maintain a healthy, pest-free environment.

"Home is a sense of belonging and identity for individuals and families."

—William Julius Wilson

Emergency Preparedness

Being prepared for emergencies is a crucial aspect of home maintenance, ensuring the safety and security of all occupants. Creating a comprehensive emergency plan, assembling an emergency kit, knowing how to shut off utilities, and maintaining fire safety measures are fundamental steps.

Creating a Home Emergency Plan

Identify Risks: Understand the types of emergencies most likely to occur in your area, such as natural disasters, power outages, or fires.

Plan Escape Routes: Create multiple escape routes from each room and designate a safe meeting spot outside your home.

Communication Plan: Establish a family communication plan. Choose an out-of-town contact, and everyone can call to check-in.

Practice Drills: Regularly practice evacuation drills with all household members. Review and update your emergency plan annually or as needed.

Essential Supplies for a Home Emergency Kit

Water and Food: Store at least one gallon of water per person daily for at least three days. Keep a three-day supply of non-perishable food items.

First Aid Kit: Include basic supplies for minor injuries, medications, and prescription items.

Flashlights and Batteries: Ensure you have working flashlights and extra batteries. Consider solar-powered or hand-crank options.

Important Documents: Keep copies of essential documents in a waterproof container. This includes IDs, insurance policies, and bank account records.

Tools and Supplies: Have tools to turn off utilities, a manual can opener, a multi-tool, and sanitation supplies.

Communication Devices: Include a battery-powered or hand-crank radio to receive emergency information. Consider portable chargers for cell phones.

How to Shut Off Your Home's Main Water, Gas, and Electricity

Water: Locate the main shut-off valve near the water meter. Turn the valve clockwise to shut it off. This is crucial to prevent flooding during a pipe burst.

Gas: Identify the main gas valve, typically outside near the gas meter. Use a wrench to turn the valve 90 degrees to the off position. Only turn off the gas if you smell gas, hear a hissing noise, or in the event of an earthquake.

Electricity: Find your home's main electrical panel. Flip the main circuit breaker to the "Off" position to cut power. This may be necessary during flooding or if you notice damaged wires.

Fire Safety Checks and Fire Extinguisher Maintenance

Smoke Detectors: Test smoke detectors monthly and replace batteries at least once a year. Install detectors in every bedroom, outside sleeping areas, and on every level of your home.

Fire Extinguishers: Keep a fire extinguisher on each floor, especially in the kitchen. Check the pressure gauge monthly to ensure it's charged and inspect for damage or corrosion.

Maintenance: Follow the manufacturer's instructions for maintenance. Most extinguishers require a professional inspection every year and recharge after use or every 6 to 12 years, even if unused.

Fire Escape Plan: Incorporate fire escape routes into your emergency plan. Practice using different exits and ensure windows are not stuck.

By taking these steps towards emergency preparedness, you can ensure that you and your family are better equipped to handle unexpected situations safely and efficiently. Regularly review and practice your emergency plans to keep everyone informed and prepared.

"A house is made of walls and beams; a home is built with love and dreams."

—William Arthur Ward

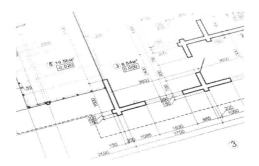

Home Improvement and Enhancements

Embarking on home improvement projects can be exciting, adding comfort, functionality, and value to your property. However, successful projects require careful planning, budgeting, and understanding when to DIY or hire a professional. Additionally, awareness of necessary permits and regulations is crucial to ensure your projects comply with local standards.

Planning and Budgeting for Home Improvement Projects

Set Clear Goals: Define what you want to achieve with your project, whether it's updating a kitchen, creating more space, or improving energy efficiency.

Research Costs: Estimate the cost of materials, labor, and any unexpected expenses. Online calculators, quotes from contractors, and price comparisons can help in this phase.

Create a Budget: Based on your research, create a realistic budget with a buffer of at least 10-20% for unforeseen costs.

Funding: Determine how you will finance the project. Options include savings, home equity loans, or personal loans. Choose the one that makes the most sense for your financial situation.

Prioritizing Projects That Add Value to Your Home

Kitchens and Bathrooms: Remodeling kitchens and bathrooms often offers the highest return on investment. Even minor updates can significantly impact your home's value.

Energy Efficiency: Upgrading to energy-efficient windows, insulation, and HVAC systems can reduce utility bills and appeal to future buyers.

Curb Appeal: Projects like exterior painting, landscaping, and door replacement can improve first impressions and boost home value.

Maintenance and Repairs: Before aesthetic improvements, ensure your home is free of maintenance issues, such as leaks, structural problems, or outdated electrical systems.

DIY vs. Hiring a Professional: Making the Right Choice

Assess Your Skills: Be realistic about your abilities and the time commitment required. Some projects, like painting, are more DIY-friendly than electrical or plumbing work.

Consider Safety and Tools: Evaluate the safety risks and whether you have the necessary tools. Renting or buying tools can add to the cost.

Cost vs. Quality: While DIY can save labor costs, consider the quality of the outcome. Professional work often comes with warranties and guarantees.

Permits and Regulations: Some projects may require permits or inspections that professionals are more familiar with.

Permits and Regulations: What You Need to Know

Research Local Requirements: Building codes and permit requirements vary by location. Check with your local building department or municipality for specific regulations.

Types of Permits: Projects that alter the structure, electrical, plumbing, or mechanical systems often require permits. Cosmetic updates like painting usually do not.

Application Process: Submit detailed project plans and pay the necessary fees. Some areas allow homeowners to apply for permits, while others may require a licensed contractor to apply.

Inspections: Most projects with permits will require one or more inspections to ensure the work complies with local codes and standards.

Successfully managing home improvement projects involves a careful balance of planning, budgeting, and execution. By prioritizing projects that add value, understanding when to DIY or hire professionals, and navigating the permit process, you can enhance your living space while optimizing your investment.

"Owning your own home is one of the best investments for your hard-earned dollars."

—Karen Weaver

Resources

A well-maintained home requires effort, dedication, and the right resources. From the essential tools for DIY tasks to online platforms for tracking maintenance schedules and from educational materials for expanding your knowledge to professional services for expert assistance, here's a comprehensive list of resources to keep your home in top condition.

Recommended Tools for Your Home Toolkit

Essential Hand Tools: Include a hammer, screwdrivers (flathead and Phillips), pliers, a tape measure, a level, and an adjustable wrench.

Power Tools: A cordless drill, a circular saw, and a sander can save time and effort for many DIY projects.

Painting Supplies: Keep quality paintbrushes, rollers, paint trays, and drop cloths on hand for touch-ups and painting projects.

Plumbing Essentials: A plunger, a pipe wrench, and a drain snake should be available to address minor plumbing issues.

Electrical Toolkit: Ensure you have wire strippers, a voltage tester, and a variety of electrical tape and connectors for essential electrical work.

Safety Gear: Always have safety glasses, gloves, ear protection, and a dust mask to protect against everyday hazards.

Online Resources and Apps for Home Maintenance Tracking

HomeZada: A comprehensive app that helps manage home improvement projects, maintenance schedules, and home finances.

Centriq: Allows users to upload appliance and device photos, providing access to user manuals, maintenance schedules, and part/order information.

BrightNest: Offers customized tips and reminders for home maintenance tasks and DIY projects based on your home's features.

Books and Guides for Deeper Learning

"Home Maintenance for Dummies" by James Carey and Morris Carey: A beginner-friendly guide covering a wide range of maintenance tasks and home improvements.

"The Complete Do-It-Yourself Manual" by Family Handyman: Offers detailed instructions for repairs, remodeling, and maintenance projects.

"New Fix-It-Yourself Manual: How to Repair, Clean, and Maintain Anything and Everything In and Around Your Home" by Reader's Digest Provides easy-to-follow instructions on fixing everyday household items.

Professional Associations and Services for When You Need to Hire Help

National Association of Home Builders (NAHB): Offers resources for finding builders and contractors who are members of their local Home Builders' Associations.

HomeAdvisor and Angie's List: Online platforms to find and vet local contractors for larger projects or repairs that require professional expertise.

Better Business Bureau (BBB): A good resource for checking local businesses and contractors' reliability and customer satisfaction ratings.

Local Trade Unions: For specialized work like electrical, plumbing, or HVAC, contact local trade unions for referrals to certified professionals.

Equipping yourself with the right tools, knowledge, and resources can make home maintenance a more manageable and rewarding part of homeownership. Whether tackling a DIY project, learning more about how to care for your home, or seeking professional help for complex tasks, these resources provide a solid foundation for keeping your home in excellent condition.

"Home is where the heart is."

—Pliny the Elder

Conclusion

Regular home maintenance is not just a set of chores; it's an investment in your home's future and a crucial aspect of homeownership. It ensures that your living space remains safe, comfortable, and efficient while preserving and potentially increasing your home's value. By understanding the importance of routine upkeep, recognizing the cost-saving benefits of proactive care, and embracing maintenance as a regular part of homeownership, you can enjoy the rewards of a well-kept home.

The Importance of Regular Home Maintenance

Regularly maintaining your home helps identify potential problems, preventing minor issues from escalating into major repairs. It extends the lifespan of critical systems and appliances, ensuring they run more efficiently and saving you from unexpected breakdowns. Regular upkeep enhances your home's curb appeal and functionality, making it a more enjoyable place to live and a more attractive proposition should you decide to sell.

How Staying Proactive Can Save Money and Prevent Emergencies

Proactive maintenance is critical to avoiding the inconvenience and expense of emergency repairs. For instance, promptly fixing a small leak can prevent costly water damage, and cleaning your dryer vent annually can reduce the fire risk. These preventive measures save on repair costs and reduce utility bills by ensuring your home's systems operate at peak efficiency. Furthermore, staying ahead of maintenance can avoid the stress and disruption of dealing with emergencies, providing peace of mind knowing your home is well cared for.

Encouragement to Make Home Maintenance a Regular Part of Homeownership

Consider home maintenance as part of the ongoing journey of homeownership. Just as you would care for a vehicle or personal health, your home requires regular attention and care to stay in its best condition. Create a maintenance schedule tailored to your home's needs, incorporating the tasks and timelines discussed in this guide. Use available resources, from tools and apps to books and professional services, to support your maintenance efforts.

Remember, the goal of home maintenance is not just about preventing problems. It's about enhancing your quality of life and securing a safe and comfortable environment for you and your loved ones. Integrating regular maintenance into your routine safeguards your investment and creates a welcoming and well-functioning home.

Regular home maintenance is a cornerstone of responsible homeownership. It requires commitment, foresight, and a proactive approach, but the rewards—financial savings, emergency prevention, and the satisfaction of a well-maintained home—are well worth the effort. Embrace the practices outlined in this guide and make home maintenance a regular and rewarding part of your life.

Appendices

How to Clean Gutters and Downspouts

Cleaning your gutters and downspouts is a vital maintenance task that protects your home's foundation, prevents water damage, and avoids costly repairs. Gutters should be cleaned at least twice a year, typically in the spring and fall, to remove leaves, debris, and other blockages. This guide will walk you through the steps to clean your gutters and downspouts safely and effectively.

Tools and Materials Needed
- Ladder (ensure it is sturdy and secure)
- Work gloves (to protect your hands)
- Bucket or plastic bag (for debris collection)
- Gutter scoop or small garden trowel
- Garden hose with a spray nozzle
- Plumber's snake or a straightened wire hanger (for tough clogs)
- Safety goggles (to protect your eyes)
- Rubber shoes (if you need to walk on the roof)

Safety Precautions
- **Ladder Safety**: Always use a stable ladder, preferably with someone to spot you. Avoid overreaching; it's safer to move the ladder frequently.
- **Wear Protective Gear**: Gloves can prevent cuts from metal edges, and goggles will protect your eyes from debris.

Cleaning Steps

1. **Prepare Your Area**: Position your ladder securely on a firm, level surface. Attach your bucket or bag to the ladder for accessible debris collection.

2. **Remove Large Debris**: Start near a downspout and remove leaves, twigs, and any large debris by hand, placing it in your bucket or bag. Work your way around the house, repositioning the ladder as necessary.

3. **Scoop Out the Smaller Debris**: Use a gutter scoop or a small garden trowel to remove smaller particles. Be gentle to avoid damaging the gutter.

4. **Flush the Gutters:** Once the debris is removed, use a garden hose to flush the gutters. This will help you identify any remaining clogs and check for proper water flow. Start from the end opposite the downspout and work your way toward it.

5. **Clear Downspouts**: They may be clogged if water isn't flowing freely through the downspouts. Insert a plumber's snake from the top down to break up clogs, or use a straightened wire hanger. Alternatively, you can flush the downspout with a hose. If the water backs up, the clog hasn't cleared.

6. **Check for Repairs**: While cleaning, inspect your gutters for signs of wear, sagging, or damage. Ensure all hangers are securely fastened. Note any leaks or holes that may need repair.

Additional Tips

- **Consider Gutter Guards**: Installing gutter guards can significantly reduce debris entering your gutters, making future cleaning easier.
- **Regular Inspections**: Even with gutter guards, inspect your gutters for damage at least once a year and thoroughly clean as needed.
- **Downspout Extensions**: Ensure downspouts extend 5 feet from your home's foundation to prevent water damage.

Cleaning your gutters and downspouts is an essential but often overlooked home maintenance task. Regular cleaning prevents water damage, protects roofing and landscaping, and extends the life of your gutters. By following this guide, you can ensure your gutter system functions correctly, keeping your home safe from water-related issues.

How to Test Smoke and Carbon Monoxide Detectors

Smoke and carbon monoxide (CO) detectors are critical safety devices in any home, designed to alert you to dangerous smoke or CO levels, potentially saving lives. Testing these detectors regularly ensures they work correctly and can provide the necessary protection in an emergency. Here's how to conduct these tests effectively.

Tools and Materials Needed
- Step ladder (if detectors are mounted high)
- Manual for the detectors (optional, but helpful for specific instructions)

Preparation
- **Know Your Detectors**: Identify whether your detectors are battery-operated, hardwired, or a combination (with battery backup).
- **Locate All Detectors**: Ensure you know the location of all smoke and CO detectors in your home.
- **Review the Manual**: If available, review the manufacturer's instructions for testing, as procedures may vary slightly.

Testing Smoke Detectors
1. **Inform Your Household**: Let everyone in your home know you will test the detectors to avoid unnecessary panic.
2. **Test Button Method**:
   - Press and hold the test button on the smoke detector.
   - Wait for the alarm to sound. It should be loud and clear.
   - Release the test button, and the alarm should stop.
3. **Smoke Method** (Optional):
   - For a more thorough test, light a match or a candle and blow it out under the detector, letting the smoke drift up.
   - The alarm should sound. If it doesn't, replace the battery (if battery-operated) or consult a professional (if hardwired).

Testing Carbon Monoxide Detectors
1. **Press the Test Button**:
    - Similar to smoke detectors, press and hold the test button on the CO detector.
    - The device should emit a loud beep or alarm sound, indicating it's functioning correctly.
2. **Check the Display** (if applicable):
    - For models with a digital display, observe any change in the readout when testing, ensuring it responds appropriately.

After Testing
- **Replace Batteries Annually**: Even if the detectors appear to be working correctly, replace the batteries at least once a year for battery-operated units. A good reminder is when you change the clocks for daylight saving time.
- **Replace Detectors as Needed**: Smoke detectors should be replaced every ten years, and CO detectors should be replaced according to the manufacturer's recommendation (usually every 5-7 years).
- **Clean Detectors**: Dust or vacuum around the detectors' openings to ensure they remain free of debris that could hinder their sensitivity.
- **Keep a Log**: Record the date of testing and battery replacements to maintain a regular maintenance schedule.

Safety Tips
- **Never Ignore Alarms**: Always act immediately if a detector goes off, even if it's believed to be a false alarm. Verify the safety of your environment first.
- **Install Detectors Strategically**: Ensure smoke and CO detectors are installed on every level of your home, including inside and outside sleeping areas.
- **Interconnected Detectors**: Consider using interconnected smoke and CO detectors so that when one sounds, they all do, providing quicker alerts throughout the home.

Regular testing of your smoke and carbon monoxide detectors is a simple yet crucial part of home safety maintenance. By following these steps, you can ensure that your detectors are always ready to alert you to potential dangers, providing peace of mind and protecting your household.

A Guide for Home Ownership

How to Seal Windows and Doors

Sealing windows and doors is an essential home maintenance task that can significantly improve energy efficiency, reduce drafts, and lower heating and cooling costs. Proper sealing prevents air leaks, keeping warm air out in the summer and winter. This guide will walk you through the steps to seal your windows and doors effectively.

Tools and Materials Needed
- Caulk and caulk gun
- Weatherstripping
- Expanding foam sealant
- Putty knife
- Scissors or a utility knife
- Tape measure
- Cleaning supplies (soap, water, and a rag)
- Paint or primer (if necessary)

Steps to Seal Windows

1. **Inspect and Clean**
   - Inspect windows for gaps or cracks where air might be escaping. Pay special attention to where the window sash meets the frame and where the frame meets the wall.
   - Clean the surfaces around the window frame. Remove any old caulk or paint with a putty knife, ensuring the area is dry and debris-free.

2. **Apply Caulk**
   - For gaps smaller than 1/4 inch, apply exterior-grade caulk around the window frame where it meets the siding or the wall. Smooth the caulk with a wet finger or a putty knife.
   - For interior gaps, especially around the window sash, use paintable caulk for a seamless finish.

3. **Install Weatherstripping**
   - Measure the perimeter of the window to determine how much weatherstripping you'll need.
   - Cut the weatherstripping to length and apply it

according to the product instructions. This typically involves peeling off a backing and pressing the adhesive side firmly.

Steps to Seal Doors

1. **Inspect and Clean**
   - Check the door frame and threshold for gaps and wear. Look for daylight or feel for drafts around the edges of the door.
   - Clean the door frame and threshold thoroughly, removing any old weatherstripping or debris.

2. **Install New Weatherstripping**
   - Measure the door frame and cut the new weatherstripping to fit. Install it around the top and sides of the door frame, ensuring a snug fit when the door is closed.
   - For the door's bottom, consider installing a door sweep if there's a gap between the door and the threshold. Cut the sweep to fit the width of your door, then screw or nail it in place so it lightly brushes against the threshold.

3. **Seal Gaps with Expanding Foam**
   - For more significant gaps around door frames, use expanding foam sealant. Be cautious, as the foam expands significantly. It's best used in areas that are hidden from view, such as behind door trim.

Additional Tips

- **Test for Leaks**: Hold a lit incense stick or a thin piece of toilet paper near windows and doors on a windy day. The smoke or paper movement can help you identify leaks.
- **Regular Maintenance**: Check the seals around windows and doors annually and reapply caulk or weatherstripping as needed.
- **Consider Energy Efficiency**: When sealing leaks, consider adding energy-efficient window films or thermal curtains to improve insulation.

Sealing windows and doors is a cost-effective way to enhance your home's comfort and energy efficiency. With the right tools and materials, you can easily tackle this project over a weekend, resulting in immediate benefits for your wallet and the environment. Regular checks and maintenance ensure your seals remain effective year-round, keeping your home cozy and draft-free.

How to Flush a Water Heater

Flushing your water heater is an essential maintenance task that helps to remove sediment buildup, which can affect the appliance's efficiency and longevity. This guide will walk you through flushing a water heater safely and effectively.

Tools and Materials Needed
- Garden hose
- Bucket (optional)
- Gloves
- Protective eyewear
- Screwdriver or wrench (if needed)

Preparation
1. Turn Off the Power: Turn off the power at the circuit breaker for electric water heaters. For gas water heaters, set the thermostat to the "pilot" setting to prevent the burners from coming on during the process.

2. Prepare the Area: Place a bucket (if using one) beneath the drain valve and run the garden hose from the valve to a suitable draining area where hot water and sediment can be safely discharged.

Flushing Process
1. Turn Off the Cold-Water Supply: Locate the cold water supply valve, usually found at the top of the water heater, and turn it off to stop more water from entering the tank.

2. Open a Hot Water Tap: Open a hot water tap nearest the water heater, preferably on the floor above. This prevents a vacuum from forming in the lines while you drain the tank.

3. Attach the Hose: Attach a garden hose to the drain valve at the water heater's bottom. Ensure the other end of the hose is in a drain or outside.

4. Open the Drain Valve: Open the drain valve to allow the water to flow out. Be careful; the water will be hot. If the water flows slowly or is blocked, opening the temperature-pressure relief valve at the top of the tank may improve flow.

5. Flush the Tank: After the tank has drained completely, turn on the cold-water supply to the tank to flush out any remaining sediment. Watch the water flowing out of the hose. When it runs clear, the tank is clean.

6. Close the Drain Valve: Once the water runs clear, close the drain valve, remove the hose, and close the temperature-pressure relief valve if you open it.

7. Refill the Tank: Turn on the cold-water supply to the tank. Go to the open hot water tap you used earlier. Once water comes out of the tap, the tank is full. At this point, you can turn off the tap.

8. Turn the Power Back On: Once the tank is full, and there's no air in the tank, turn the power back on for electric water heaters. For gas water heaters, turn the gas valve back to the "on" position and relight the pilot light, if necessary, according to the manufacturer's instructions.

Post-Flushing Checks
- Check for leaks around the drain valve.
- Monitor the water heater for unusual noises in the first few hours after flushing.
- Ensure the water temperature returns to normal before using hot water appliances.

Flushing your water heater annually can significantly extend its life and efficiency. If you encounter issues during the flushing process or if the water heater shows signs of malfunction afterward, consider consulting a professional plumber. Regular maintenance, including flushing, helps prevent corrosion, heating element failure, and other common water heater problems.

Checking and Replacing the Water Heater Anode Rod

The anode rod is a crucial component of your water heater that prevents rusting inside the tank. Also known as a sacrificial rod, it attracts corrosive elements in the water, thereby protecting the tank walls. Over time, the anode rod deteriorates and must be checked regularly to determine if a replacement is necessary. Here's how to inspect and replace the anode rod in your water heater.

Tools and Materials Needed
- Socket wrench
- Pipe wrench (if needed)
- Replacement anode rod (if necessary)
- Teflon tape
- Gloves
- Protective eyewear

Preparation
- Safety First: Ensure the power to the water heater is turned off (electricity at the circuit breaker or gas supply turned to "pilot").
- Access: Ensure you have clear access to the top of the water heater where the anode rod is located.

Checking the Anode Rod
1. Locate the Anode Rod: The anode rod is usually found at the top of the water heater. It may be directly visible or located under a cap on the top of the tank.

2. Remove the Anode Rod: Use a socket wrench to loosen the anode rod. If it's particularly tight, you may need a pipe wrench for additional leverage. Carefully remove the rod from the tank.

3. Inspect the Rod: Check the condition of the anode rod. If it's heavily eroded, less than 1/2 inch thick, or covered in calcium, it's time to replace it. A little corrosion is typical, which means the rod is doing its job.

Replacing the Anode Rod

1. Purchase the Correct Rod: Anode rods come in different sizes and materials (aluminum, magnesium, and zinc). Ensure you buy one that matches your water heater's specifications and local water conditions.

2. Prepare the New Rod: If the new anode rod is too tall for your space, you may need to bend or cut it to fit. Some rods are designed with segments for this purpose.

3. Apply Teflon Tape: Wrap Teflon tape around the threads of the new rod to ensure a good seal and prevent leaks.

4. Install the New Rod: Carefully insert the new anode rod into the tank and tighten it with the socket wrench. Do not over-tighten it, but ensure it is secure to prevent leaks.

5. Restore Power and Check for Leaks: Once the new rod is in place, turn the power back on to the water heater and check around the anode rod for any signs of leaks.

Maintenance Tips

- Frequency of Checks: It's a good practice to check the anode rod every 2-3 years, but this may vary based on your water quality and water heater usage.
- Early Replacement Benefits: Replacing the anode rod before it's completely corroded can significantly extend your water heater's life.
- Professional Inspection: If you're unsure about the condition of your anode rod or how to replace it, consider hiring a professional plumber for an inspection.

By maintaining the anode rod, you're taking a crucial step in prolonging your water heater's life and ensuring it runs efficiently. Regular checks and timely replacement of the anode rod can prevent rust and corrosion inside the tank, safeguarding your home's hot water supply.

How to Change HVAC Air Filters

Changing the air filters in your HVAC system is a simple yet crucial maintenance task that improves air quality, increases system efficiency, and extends the life of your HVAC unit. A clean air filter ensures optimal airflow, reducing energy costs and preventing dust, allergens, and other pollutants from circulating through your home. Here's how to change your HVAC air filters effectively.

Tools and Materials Needed
- New air filter (make sure it's the correct size)
- Screwdriver (if required to open the HVAC unit cover)
- Gloves (optional, to keep your hands clean)
- A bag for the old filter (to prevent dust from spreading)

Steps to Change Your HVAC Air Filter

1. **Locate Your Air Filter**
   - Air filters can be found in various places depending on your HVAC system: in a slot on the HVAC unit itself, behind a return air grille on a wall or ceiling, or inside the blower compartment. If you're unsure, consult your HVAC system's manual.

2. **Turn Off the HVAC System**
   - Before changing the filter, ensure the system is off to prevent unfiltered air from circulating through the system and your home.

3. **Remove the Old Filter**
   - Open or remove the cover to the filter compartment. Note the direction of the airflow arrow and the size marked on the filter's edge before removing it. This is crucial for installing the new filter correctly.
   - Carefully slide the filter out of the slot or compartment.

4. **Check the Condition**
   - Inspect the old filter. If it's visibly dirty, covered in dust, pet hair, or debris, it's time for a change. Even if it looks relatively clean, a standard rule is to replace HVAC filters every 90 days for 1-3 inch filters and every 6-12 months for 4-5 inch filters.

5. **Insert the New Filter**
   - Take the new filter out of its packaging. Make sure it's the correct size and type for your system.
   - Look for the airflow arrow on the side of the filter. This arrow should point in the direction of airflow, typically away from the return air duct and toward the HVAC unit.
   - Slide the filter into place carefully, ensuring it fits snugly without gaps around the edges.

6. **Replace the Cover and Turn the System On**
   - Once the new filter is in place, replace any covers or doors you had to open or remove.
   - Turn your HVAC system back on. Consider setting a reminder for the following filter change.

Tips for Maintaining Your HVAC Air Filters

- **Keep Spare Filters**: Having extra filters on hand makes it easy to change them regularly without delay.
- **Regular Checks**: Especially during high-use seasons, check your filters monthly. Pets, construction nearby, or high pollen counts can increase filter clogging.
- **Understand Filter Ratings**: Filters have ratings for MERV (Minimum Efficiency Reporting Value). Higher MERV ratings indicate finer filtration, which is beneficial for capturing more and smaller particles. However, ensure your system can handle the airflow restriction higher MERV filters may cause.

Regularly changing your HVAC air filters is a key aspect of home maintenance that shouldn't be overlooked. By following these simple steps, you can improve your home's air quality, enhance the efficiency of your HVAC system, and ensure a healthier living environment for you and your family. This routine task not only contributes to the longevity of your HVAC system but also helps in reducing your energy bills by maintaining optimal system performance. Embrace this practice as a part of your regular home care routine to breathe easier and enjoy the comfort of your home to its fullest.

How to Fix a Leaky Faucet

A leaky faucet is not just a nuisance; it can lead to wasted water and increased utility bills. Fortunately, with a few tools and some know-how, fixing a leaky faucet is a manageable DIY project for most homeowners. This guide will walk you through the typical steps to diagnose and repair a dripping faucet.

Tools and Materials Needed
- Adjustable wrench or set of wrenches
- Screwdrivers (flathead and Phillips)
- Replacement washers and O-rings (specific to your faucet type)
- Plumber's tape
- Rag or towel
- Penetrating oil (such as WD-40, if necessary)
- Bucket or container (to catch water)

Identifying the Faucet Type
The first step in fixing a leaky faucet is identifying its type, which determines the repair process. The most common types include:
- Compression faucets: These have two handles, one for hot and one for cold, and work by compressing a rubber washer to stop water flow.
- Cartridge (sleeve) faucets: Can have one or two handles. Inside, a cartridge controls the water flow.
- Ceramic-disk faucets: Feature a single handle and use a ceramic cylinder that regulates water flow.
- Ball-type faucets: These have a single handle that moves over a ball-shaped cap right above the base of the faucet.

Steps for Repair

1. **Turn Off the Water Supply**
   - Locate the shut-off valves under the sink and turn them clockwise to shut off the water supply to the faucet. Open the faucet to drain any remaining water and relieve pressure.

2. **Disassemble the Faucet**
   - Place a rag or towel around the drain to prevent small parts from falling in.

- Use the appropriate screwdriver to remove the handle(s). You might need to remove a decorative cap to access the screw.
- Take note of the assembly order as you disassemble the faucet to ensure proper reassembly.

3. **Inspect and Replace Faulty Parts**
   - **For Compression Faucets**: Look for a worn-out washer at the base of the stem. Replace it with a new one that matches in size and shape.
   - **For Cartridge Faucets**: Carefully remove the cartridge. You may need to replace the entire cartridge or just the O-rings.
   - **For Ceramic-Disk Faucets**: Take out the ceramic disk and clean it. If the leak persists, replace the seals or the entire disk.
   - **For Ball-Type Faucets**: These are more complex due to the number of parts. Consider buying a replacement kit that includes all the parts you might need.

4. **Clean and Reassemble**
   - Clean any sediment or debris from the faucet components. Use penetrating oil to loosen any challenging parts.
   - Reassemble the faucet in the reverse order of disassembly. Apply the plumber's tape to any threaded parts to ensure a good seal.
   - Replace any worn O-rings or seals as you reassemble.

5. **Test the Faucet**
   - Turn the water supply back on by turning the shut-off valves counterclockwise. Check the faucet for leaks.
   - If the faucet still leaks, double-check your work, ensuring all parts are correctly installed and secure. It may be necessary to replace additional components.

Fixing a leaky faucet is a satisfying and environmentally responsible DIY project that can save water and reduce utility bills. By following these steps and understanding the basics of faucet types, you can confidently tackle the most common leaks. Always work carefully and keep track of all parts during disassembly to ensure a successful repair.

How to Unclog Drains

Clogged drains are a common household issue that can lead to water backup and potential water damage if not addressed promptly. From kitchen sinks to bathroom drains, clogs can occur for various reasons, including accumulated hair, grease, soap scum, and foreign objects. This guide will provide practical methods to unclog drains using tools and ingredients you likely already have at home.

Tools and Materials Needed
- Plunger
- Baking soda and vinegar
- Boiling water
- Plumber's snake or wire hanger
- Wet/dry vacuum (optional)
- Rubber gloves
- Bucket and rags for cleanup

Methods to Unclog Drains

Method 1: Boiling Water
This is the simplest method and is often effective for minor clogs caused by soap or grease.
1. Boil a kettle of water.
2. Pour the boiling water directly down the drain in two to three stages, allowing the hot water to work between each pour.

Method 2: Baking Soda and Vinegar
It is an eco-friendly method that uses the chemical reaction between baking soda and vinegar to clear clogs.
1. Pour half a cup of baking soda directly into the drain.
2. Follow with half a cup of white vinegar.
3. Cover the drain with a plug or rag to keep the reaction below the surface, enhancing its effectiveness.
4. Wait an hour or overnight for the best results, then flush with hot water.

Method 3: Plunging
A plunger can create enough suction to dislodge blockages, especially in toilets and sinks.
1. Fill the sink or tub with enough water to cover the plunger's head.

2. Place the plunger over the drain and pump vigorously for about 20 seconds.
3. Pull the plunger off the drain opening to break the air seal. The water should rush down, indicating the clog is cleared.

Method 4: Plumber's Snake or Wire Hanger
This method is effective for physical removal of blockages, such as hair or foreign objects.
1. Straighten a wire hanger, leaving a small hook at one end.
2. Push the hook end into the drain and twist to catch and pull out debris. Alternatively, insert a plumber's snake into the drain, extending it until you feel resistance, then twist and pull.
3. flush the drain with hot water once the debris is cleared.

Method 5: Wet/Dry Vacuum
A wet/dry vacuum can be set to wet mode to suck out clogs if you have one available.
1. Using the vacuum's nozzle, Create a tight seal over the drain.
2. Turn the vacuum to its highest setting to draw the clog out.
3. After attempting to vacuum the clog, flush the drain with water to check if the clog is cleared.

Tips for Preventing Future Clogs
- Use strainers in your sinks to catch hair and food particles.
- Avoid pouring grease or oil down kitchen drains.
- Regularly flush drains with boiling water or a baking soda and vinegar mixture to keep them clear.
- Be mindful of what you flush down toilets, stick to human waste and toilet paper only.

Clogged drains are a nuisance but can often be resolved without professional help. Using the methods outlined in this guide, you can tackle clogs effectively and keep your drains running smoothly. Remember, prevention is critical to avoiding future clogs, so take proactive measures to keep your plumbing system in optimal condition. Regular maintenance and mindful usage are the cornerstones of ensuring that your home remains free from the hassles of blocked pipes and the potential for water damage. Embrace these practices, and enjoy a home that's as functional as it is comfortable, with drains that are clear and fully operational.

How to Patch and Repair Drywall

Repairing drywall is a crucial skill for homeowners, as it's common for walls to suffer from dings, holes, or water damage over time. Whether you're dealing with a small hole from a nail or a larger area that needs patching, this guide will walk you through the process step-by-step.

Tools and Materials Needed
- Drywall patch or mesh tape
- Joint compound (drywall mud)
- Putty knife
- Sandpaper (fine grit)
- Primer and paint
- Drywall saw or utility knife (for more extensive repairs)
- Drywall or a scrap piece (for larger holes)

For Small Holes (e.g., Nail Holes)
1. Prepare the Surface: Ensure the area around the hole is clean and dry. Remove any loose debris or paper around the hole.
2. Apply Joint Compound: Using a putty knife, fill the hole with joint compound. Smooth it out so it's flush with the wall.
3. Let It Dry: Allow the compound to dry completely, following the manufacturer's recommended drying time.
4. Sand Smooth: Lightly sand the area until smooth once dry.
5. Paint: Prime the repaired area before applying paint that matches the surrounding wall.

For Medium Holes (e.g., Doorknob Damage)
1. Clean the Area: Trim any frayed edges or loose paper around the hole.
2. Apply Patch: Use a self-adhesive mesh patch for holes up to a few inches wide. Place the patch over the hole, pressing firmly.
3. Cover with Joint Compound: Apply a thin layer of joint compound over the patch with a putty knife, extending slightly beyond the patch's edges. Let it dry.
4. Apply Additional Coats: Once the first layer is dry, apply one or two more layers, letting each layer dry and sanding between coats.

5. Final Sanding and Painting: Sand the final coat smooth, then prime and paint the area.

For Larger Holes
1. Cut the Damaged Area: Use a drywall saw or utility knife to cut out the damaged area, making a square or rectangular shape.
2. Install a Support: Cut a piece of wood (like a 1x2 or plywood) longer than the hole's width. Insert it into the hole and secure it with screws through the drywall into each end of the wood. This will support the patch.
3. Cut a Drywall Patch: Measure and cut a piece of drywall to fit the hole. Screw it into the wooden support you installed.
4. Tape the Edges: Apply mesh tape around the patch's edges.
5. Apply Joint Compound: Cover the patch and tape it with the joint compound, feathering the edges. Let it dry, then apply a second coat if necessary.
6. Sand and Paint: Sand the area smooth, prime, and paint to match the wall.

Tips for a Successful Repair
- Patience Is Key: Allow the joint compound to dry thoroughly between coats to prevent cracks and uneven surfaces.
- Smooth Application: Use wide strokes with the putty knife for a smooth, feathered finish that blends with the rest of the wall.
- Match the Texture: If your walls have texture, replicate it on the patched area using specialized tools or techniques before painting.

NOTE: Several self-adhesive drywall patch products (metal, paper, or plastic drywall patches) may work for your application. Consult the manufacturer guidelines to determine whether these products will suit your needs.

Drywall repair is a valuable skill that can save homeowners time and money. With the right tools and practice, you can seamlessly repair walls, maintaining the beauty and integrity of your home's interior.

How to Care for Lawn and Garden

A lush lawn and a vibrant garden are the pride of any homeowner, offering a beautiful and tranquil outdoor space. Proper care and maintenance are essential for their health and growth. This guide will help you understand the basic needs of your lawn and garden, providing practical advice to keep them flourishing.

Understanding Your Lawn and Garden

1. **Know Your Soil**: Soil type affects water retention, nutrient availability, and pH balance. Test your soil to understand its needs better—whether it's more organic matter, lime to adjust pH or specific nutrients.

2. **Choose the Right Plants**: Choose plants suited to your climate, soil type, and the sunlight your garden receives. Native plants are often more resistant to pests and diseases and require less water.

Lawn Care

1. **Mowing**: Keep your lawn at an optimal height, which varies by grass type but is generally between 2.5 to 3.5 inches. Mow regularly, never removing more than one-third of the grass blade length to avoid stress on the grass.

2. **Watering**: Lawns typically need about 1 inch of water per week, including rainfall. It's best to water deeply and infrequently to encourage profound root growth. Morning watering is ideal to reduce evaporation and fungal diseases.

3. **Fertilizing**: Use a fertilizer suited to your grass type and soil needs. Slow-release fertilizers nourish your lawn over time and reduce the risk of over-fertilization.

4. **Aerating**: Aerating your lawn once a year helps relieve soil compaction, allowing water, air, and nutrients to reach the roots more easily.

5. **Overseeding**: Overseeding can introduce new growth if your lawn looks thin or patchy. Do this in the fall for cool-season grasses and late spring for warm-season grasses.

Garden Care

1. **Planting**: Plant at the right time according to the needs of each species. Ensure proper spacing to prevent overcrowding and competition for nutrients.

2. **Watering**: Gardens usually require watering once or twice a week, more frequently in hot, dry weather. Water at the base of the plants early in the morning to reduce evaporation and leaf wetness.

3. **Mulching**: Apply a 2-3 inch layer of mulch around your plants to retain moisture, regulate soil temperature, and reduce weed growth.

4. **Weeding**: Regularly remove weeds that compete with your plants for nutrients and water. Pulling them by hand is often the most effective method.

5. **Pruning**: Prune dead or diseased branches to keep plants healthy. Pruning also encourages fruiting and flowering in many species.

6. **Pest and Disease Management**: Monitor your plants for signs of pests and diseases. Use organic methods like neem oil or insecticidal soaps as a first line of defense to minimize harm to beneficial insects.

Seasonal Tips

Spring:
- Clean up debris from winter.
- Start seedlings indoors.
- Begin regular lawn mowing and fertilization.

Summer:
- Continue mowing and watering as needed.
- Harvest vegetables and flowers.
- Apply mulch to keep roots cool and moist.

Fall:
- Aerate and overseed the lawn.
- Plant bulbs for spring bloom.
- Clean up fallen leaves and prepare plants for winter.

Winter:
- Protect sensitive plants with covers or bring them indoors.
- Plan next year's garden.
- Maintain tools and equipment.

Caring for your lawn and garden is a rewarding activity that enhances your home's curb appeal and provides a serene retreat. Regular maintenance and attention to the specific needs of your plants and lawn will ensure they remain healthy and vibrant throughout the year. Patience and consistent care are vital to cultivating a thriving outdoor space.

How to Maintain a Deck or Patio

Maintaining your deck or patio is essential for extending its life and keeping it safe and enjoyable for outdoor activities. Regular care and maintenance can prevent damage and costly repairs, whether you have a wooden deck, a concrete patio, or composite decking. This guide will provide practical steps to maintain your deck or patio throughout the year.

Tools and Materials Needed

- Broom and garden hose or pressure washer (with appropriate settings for your deck material)
- Deck cleaner or mild detergent
- Stiff brush or scrubbing pad
- Sandpaper (for wood decks)
- Sealant, stain, or paint (for wood decks)
- Concrete sealer (for concrete patios)
- Protective gear (gloves, eye protection)

General Cleaning
(Applicable to All Types of Decks and Patios)

1. **Remove Furniture and Debris**: Clear the deck or patio of furniture, grills, and potted plants. Sweep to remove loose debris, leaves, and dirt.
2. **Wash the Surface**: Using a garden hose with a spray nozzle or a pressure washer set to a gentle spray, wash the surface to remove dirt and grime. Use a deck cleaner or a mild detergent solution for stubborn stains and scrub with a stiff brush.
3. **Rinse Thoroughly**: Rinse the deck or patio with clean water to remove any soap residue.

Maintenance of Wood Decks

1. **Inspect Annually**: Check for loose nails, splintered wood, or rotting boards. Tighten, sand, or replace as necessary.
2. **Clean Regularly**: Use a wood deck cleaner once a year to remove mold, mildew, and built-up grime. Follow the product instructions for the best results.
3. **Sand Rough Areas**: If you notice splinters or rough patches, sand these areas smoothly to prevent injuries.
4. **Apply Sealant, Stain, or Paint**: After cleaning and drying, apply a water-repellent sealant or stain to protect the wood from moisture. If preferred, paint the wood with a

product designed for outdoor decks. This should be done every 2-3 years, depending on weather conditions and the product used.

Maintenance of Composite Decks
1. **Follow Manufacturer's Guidelines**: Use cleaning and maintenance products recommended by the manufacturer to avoid damaging the composite material.
2. **Spot Treat Stains**: Address spills and stains promptly to prevent them from setting in.
3. **Avoid Power Washing**: If using a pressure washer, keep it at a low setting to prevent damaging the surface.

Maintenance of Concrete Patios
1. **Remove Stains Immediately**: Treat oil, grease, and other stains immediately with a degreaser or concrete cleaning product.
2. **Seal the Concrete**: Apply a concrete sealer every 2-3 years to protect against moisture and wear. Ensure the patio is clean and dry before applying the sealer.
3. **Repair Cracks**: Use a concrete filler or patching compound to repair any cracks or chips in the surface to prevent further damage.

Seasonal Maintenance Tips
- **Spring**: Inspect your deck or patio for any winter damage. Clean thoroughly to prepare for the outdoor season.
- **Summer**: Regularly sweep to remove debris and clean spills promptly to prevent stains.
- **Fall**: Remove leaves and debris to prevent mold and mildew growth.
- **Winter** (for applicable areas): Remove snow and ice carefully, using products that won't damage the deck or patio surface.

Maintaining your deck or patio requires regular cleaning and periodic repairs to keep it looking its best and to ensure it remains a safe, enjoyable space for outdoor living. These maintenance steps can protect your investment and you'll enjoy your outdoor space for many years.

How to Remove Gum from Carpet

Of all the substances that can sully a carpet, gum is one that seems to cause the most grief. Put down those scissors—there are better ways to get chewing gum out of the carpet than cutting it out! Below are three methods of gum removal.

Removing Gum via The Ice Cube Method

To prevent a sticky situation from getting even stickier, give lodged-in gum wads the cold shoulder—with ice cubes! This is why it pays to always keep ice on hand. Gather ice cubes from the freezer, and then complete the following steps:

- Place a couple of ice cubes in a plastic bag. Press the bag of ice onto the offending gum wad. Leave the ice on the gum for at least 1 minute. This will freeze and harden the gum, making it easier to lift off.
- Gently pick at and pull the frozen gum from the carpet using your fingers, a scraping tool, or a butter knife.
- Start lifting along the edges and move toward the center of the wad, taking care not to remove the carpet fibers along with the gum! (Master this technique, and in the future, you can even apply it to upholstery messes and gummed-up clothes.)
- At this point, most of the gum should be out of sight and out of mind, but if stubborn residue remains, root it out with a few drops of a rub featuring methyl salicylate (such as the pain-relieving cream Bengay).
- Scrub away any discoloration or carpet stains left in the gum's wake with a mild carpet-cleaning detergent.
- Rinse the area with warm water to send your gummy ordeal packing!

The WD-40 Method to Remove Chewing Gum

Another household workhorse, WD-40, is also effective for getting gum out of carpets and rugs. Chewing gum is hydrophobic, which means it can't be dissolved by water. To break it up, dissolve it using another hydrophobic material, like WD-40. (The WD-40 technique should be a quicker fix than the ice technique because you won't have to wait around for the gum to harden.) Here's what to do:

- Spray a liberal amount of WD-40 on the chewing gum stain. Point the spray straw as close as you can to the underside of the area where the gum meets the carpet. You may need to use your fingers to work the WD-40 into the carpet fibers.
- Wait 5 or 10 minutes.
- Using a rag or small scrub brush, wipe or lightly scrub the gum in one direction.
- Add more WD-40 as needed to remove remaining gum from the carpet. Continue wiping in the same direction.

The Vinegar Method

White vinegar has so many uses around the home that it's no surprise it can also be used to get gum out of carpet. Here's how to put natural, do-everything vinegar can get chewing gum from carpet:

- Warm ¼ cup of white vinegar in the microwave.
- Dab a clean white cloth or towel into the vinegar, and then dab it onto the gum.
- Use a putty knife, dull knife, or the side of a spoon to scrape away as much gum as you can.
- Use an old toothbrush to brush away the remaining gum. (The gum remnants will gunk up the toothbrush entirely, so you'll want to toss it after using it for this task.)

FAQs About How to Get Gum Out of Carpet

Q. How do you get old black gum out of carpet?
Freeze it off. Place a couple of ice cubes in a plastic bag, and leave the ice on the gum until the gum is hard and brittle. Scrape off frozen gum residue with a putty knife or butter knife.

Q. How do you get gum out of a wool carpet?
The freezing tip mentioned above will also work on removing gum stuck in wool carpets. Simply freeze the gum and scrape it off with a sharp edge, without having to worry about whether a solvent will damage the wool.

Q. How do you get chewy sweets out of carpet?
Begin by blotting the candy with a rag dipped in cold water, which should loosen the sticky bond. Scrape away any large bits of candy, and then apply a stain remover or carpet cleaning

solution. Wait a few minutes, then carefully blot the stain remover. If the stain persists, blot the stain with a clean cloth dipped in white vinegar.

Q. How do you get hard stuff out of carpet?
It depends on what the hard stuff is. If you know the substance is candle wax, you can either try the ice technique above, or use a warm iron. To remove the wax with an iron, lay a damp white cloth over the stain. Then, with an iron set to low heat, iron the cloth until it absorbs the wax. Repeat as needed, covering the wax with a clean portion of the cloth each time.

Monthly Maintenance Checklist
Month _____ Year _____

Task	Complete Date	Note
Test smoke and carbon monoxide detectors.		
Clean or replace HVAC air filters.		
Inspect and clean range hood filters.		
Check for leaks under sinks and around toilets.		
Run water and flush toilets in unused spaces.		
Inspect electrical cords for wear.		

A Guide for Home Ownership

Seasonal Maintenance Checklist
SPRING: Year _ _ _ _ _

Task	Complete Date	Note
Service HVAC system.		
Clean gutters and downspouts.		
Inspect roof for damage.		
Power wash siding and windows.		
Aerate and fertilize lawn.		
Check exterior paint and touch up as needed.		

Seasonal Maintenance Checklist
SUMMER: Year _ _ _ _ _

Task	Complete Date	Note
Check irrigation system and adjust sprinkler		
Clean or replace HVAC filters (if not monthly).		
Inspect and repair deck or patio as needed.		
Trim trees and shrubs.		
Check for pests and apply treatments if necessary.		

A Guide for Home Ownership

Seasonal Maintenance Checklist
FALL: Year _ _ _ _ _

Task	Complete Date	Note
Clean gutters and downspouts (again, after leaves fall).		
Have heating system serviced.		
Seal gaps around doors and windows to prevent drafts.		
Winterize outdoor faucets and irrigation system.		
Rake leaves and aerate the lawn.		
Inspect and clean the chimney and fireplace.		

Seasonal Maintenance Checklist
WINTER: Year _ _ _ _ _

Task	Complete Date	Note
Check insulation and weather stripping.		
Protect pipes from freezing in cold weather.		
Test sump pump.		
Inspect for ice dams and icicles.		
Keep sidewalks and entrances clear of ice and snow.		
Monitor indoor humidity levels.		

Annual Maintenance Checklist
Year _____

Task	Complete Date	Note
Drain and flush water heater.		
Inspect and possibly replace sacrificial anode rod in water heater		
Clean dryer vent duct.		
Seal tile grout.		
Clean and inspect home exterior, including siding, foundation, chimney.		
Service major appliances		

Home Safety and Security Checklist
Date: ___/___/___

Task	Complete Date	Note
Ensure all locks on doors and windows function properly.		
Check that fire extinguishers are accessible and not expired.		
Review and practice emergency evacuation plans.		
Secure heavy furniture and appliances to walls to prevent tipping.		
Test ground fault circuit interrupter (GFCI) outlets.		

Energy Efficiency Checklist
Date: ___/___/___

Task	Complete Date	Note
Seal leaks in doors, windows, and around pipes and vents.		
Install or check insulation in key areas like attics, walls, and basements.		
Use energy-efficient LED bulbs.		
Consider smart thermostats for more efficient heating and cooling.		
Perform an energy audit to identify further improvements.		

Must-Know Hacks for a Better Home Life

Cleaning Hacks

General Cleaning
- Combine cleaning tasks - clean baseboards when vacuuming floors, clean blinds when cleaning windows, etc.
- Buy a soap dispenser dish brush to use for cleaning the shower
- Use a pillowcase to clean ceiling fans
- Microwave a damp cloth with dish soap to use for cleaning grease off kitchen cabinets
- Use a Magic Eraser to clean ceramic stovetops, shower walls, floor tile, etc.

Dusting
- Dust with a Swiffer floor mop on walls and trim
- Use tongs wrapped in rags to clean blinds
- Use a paintbrush to brush dirt out from furniture
- Use coffee filters for dusting
- Use dryer sheets wrapped around a paint roller and extension pole to dust ceilings and high places

Vacuuming
- Vacuum the room horizontally first, then vertically to get all dirt
- Vacuum slowly and methodically
- Vacuum bathroom before scrubbing to eliminate hairs and dust in cleaning water

Floors
- Skip the bucket when mopping - use a spray bottle and microfiber mop instead
- Use citrus cleaner like Goo Gone to remove tree sap from vinyl siding
- Apply rain repellant like Rain-X to shower doors to prevent mineral buildup

Glass
- Clean with 1 part water, 1 part vinegar, 2 drops essential oil, and rubbing alcohol
- Remove hard water stains from faucets with half a lemon

Grout
- Use a bleach pen to clean grout lines

Trash Cans
- Use liquid toilet bowl cleaner and toilet brush to scrub the insides
- Put holes in the bottom to eliminate vacuum seals and stuck bags

Washing Machine
- Wash lint trap covers from dryer vents

Organizing Hacks

Cleaning Tools
- Store styling tools in a magazine rack
- Use over-the-door shoe organizers to store spray bottles and cleaning supplies
- Store plastic bags in used disinfectant wipes containers

Closets
- Box or bag items on shelves
- Cover rarely worn clothes with garment bags
- Keep closet floors clear for easier vacuuming

Fridge
- Use plastic tubing to fill the gap between the counter and fridge to catch fallen items

Toiletries
- Use a silverware tray to organize bathroom essentials
- Hang extra toilet paper rolls on the inside of the cabinet door with shower curtain rings
- Use a tension rod to hang shower supplies in mesh bags

Bedding
- Use suspenders clipped to corners under the mattress to keep fitted sheets in place

Painting Supplies
- Store paint brushes in tall vases or jars
- Save excess paint in mason jars
- Wrap rubber bands around a paint can rim to wipe excess paint off the brush

Hardware
- Attach magnetic tape to the hammer handle to hold the nails

Documents
- Scan documents and store digitally to reduce paper clutter

Garage/Basement
- Use shelving units and storage bins to organize seasonal items
- Label storage bins and shelves with contents

Wrapping Paper
- Store rolls of wrapping paper in a garment bag in the coat closet

Craft Supplies
- Organize by type and project in clear plastic bins so contents are visible

Pet Care Hacks

Cleaning
- Brush pets with a vacuum hose attachment to capture fur
- Remove pet fur from furniture with a squeegee
- Use duct tape rolled sticky-side out on a paint roller to remove pet fur from furniture

Litter Box
- Line with a plastic bag for easy cleaning
- Cut an opening in a storage bin for DIY covered litter box

Repair Hacks

Walls
- Cover alarms, smoke detectors, etc., with shower caps
- Put masking tape on plaster walls before nailing to prevent cracks

Furniture
- Remove crayon marks from walls with a hair dryer
- Use toothpaste to buff minor scratches out of wood furniture
- Remove candle wax from furniture with ice cubes

Carpet
- Get candle wax out with an iron and brown paper bag

Windows
- Fix small holes in screens with clear nail polish

Plants
- Use cut-up straws to support drooping flowers

Safety Hacks

Childproofing
- Use rubber bands around doorknobs to keep doors from fully closing and locking

Prevent Bruising
- Apply foam pipe insulation to corners of furniture
- Use pool noodle strips on inside car doors to prevent dinging walls

Prevent Slipping
- Apply furniture sliders under heavy flower pots
- Apply caulk strips to the bottom of the rugs

Smell/Health Hacks

Good Smells
- Simmer cinnamon sticks and vanilla beans in water to scent home
- Microwave lemon water to deodorize the microwave
- Place dryer sheets in AC vents

Cleaning Product Alternatives
- Clean with baking soda, vinegar, lemon juice, etc., instead of harsh chemicals
- Look for plant-based, non-toxic cleaning alternatives

Air Quality
- Vacuum out HVAC vents
- Run furnace fan to filter air while cleaning
- Consider removing carpeting and using hard flooring to reduce dust

Prevent Mold
- Clean the bathroom exhaust fan cover in the dishwasher
- Always run the bathroom fan when showering

"Home is the ultimate evidence of freedom. Owning your own roof over your head is the ultimate practice of independence, of freedom, and of security."

—Margaret Chase Smith

Made in the USA
Middletown, DE
12 March 2024

50890602R00051